D1566848

# Voice Culture

SonLight Education Ministry
United States of America

# A Suggested Daily Schedule

(Adapt this schedule to your family needs.)

5:00 a.m.  Arise–Personal Worship

6:00 a.m.  Family Worship and Bible Class–With Father

7:00 a.m.  Breakfast

8:00 a.m.  Practical Arts*–Domestic Activities
                                        Agriculture
                                        Industrial Arts
                                        (especially those related to
                                        the School Lessons)

10:00 a.m.  School Lessons
(Take a break for some physical exercise
during this time slot.)

12:00 p.m.  Dinner Preparations
(Health class could be included at this time
or a continued story.)

1:00 p.m.  Dinner

2:00 p.m.  Practical Arts* or Fine Arts
(Music and Crafts)
(especially those related to
the School Lessons)

5:00 p.m.  Supper

6:00 p.m.  Family Worship–Father
(Could do History Class)

7:00 p.m.  Personal time with God–Bed Preparation

8:00 p.m.  Bed

*Daily nature walk can be in morning or afternoon.

# The Desire of All Nations

This book is a part of a curriculum that is built upon the life of Christ entitled, "The Desire of All Nations," for grades 2-8. Any of the books in this curriculum can be used by themselves or as an entire program.

## INFORMATION ABOUT THE 2-8 GRADE PROGRAM

## Multi-level

This program is written on a multi-level. That means that each booklet has material for grades 2-8. This is so the whole family in these grades may work from the same books. It is difficult for a busy mother to have 2 or more children and each have a different set of books. Remember, the Bible is written for all ages.

## The Bible—the Primary Textbook

The books in this program are designed to teach the parent and the student how to learn academic subjects by using the Bible as a primary textbook.

## The Desire of Ages

*The Desire of Ages* by Ellen G. White is used as a textbook to go with the Bible. This focuses on the early life of Christ, when He was a child. Children relate best to Christ as a child and youth.

## Lesson Numbers

The big number in the top right corner on the cover of this book is the Lesson Number and corresponds with the chapter number in the book *The Desire of Ages*. For example, Lesson 1 in the school program will go along with chapter 1 in *The Desire of Ages*. Usually each family starts at the beginning with Lesson 1. Most children have not had a true Bible program, therefore they need the foundation built. If there is academic material that they have already covered, they do the Bible part and review then pass quickly on.

## Seven Academic Subjects

There are seven academic subjects in this program—Health, Mathematics, Music, Science–Nature, History/Geography/Prophecy, Language, Voice–Speech.

## Language Program

A good, solid language program is recommended to be used along with the SonLight materials.

The Riggs Institute has a multi-sensory teaching method that accommodates every child's unique learning style. Their program is called *Writing and Spelling Road to Reading and Thinking*. Order by calling (800) 200-4840 or visit www.riggsinst.org. (Disclaimer: SonLight does not endorse the reading books recommended in the Riggs' program.)

Another option which you might find more user friendly and is similar to the Riggs program but from a Christian perspective is *Spell to Write and Read* by Wanda Sanseri. To order, call Wanda Sanseri at (503) 654-2300 or visit https://www.bhibooks.net/swr.html

# "The Fullness of Time"
## Lesson 3 – Alertness

The following books are those you will need for this lesson.
All of these can be obtained from www.sonlighteducation.com

**The Rainbow Covenant** – Study the spiritual meaning of colors and make your own rainbow book.

**Health**
*The Heart*

**Math**
*Addition I*

**Music**
*Musical and Non Musical Sounds*

**Science/Nature**
*Stars and Constellations*

**A Casket** – Coloring book and story. Learn how to treat the gems of the Bible.

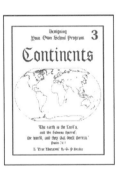

**H/G/P**
*Continents*

**Language**
*History of the Word*

**Speech/Voice**
*Voice Culture*

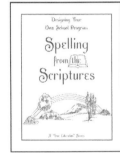

***Spelling from the Scriptures***

**Bible Study** – Learn how to study the Bible and helpful use tools.

**Bible**
*The Desire of all Nations I Teacher Study Guide*

*Student Study Guide*

*Bible Lesson Study Guide*

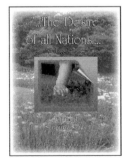

**Memory Verses**
*The Desire of all Nations I Scripture Songs Book*

*and MP3 files*

***Our Nature Study Book*** – Your personal nature journal.

# Table of Contents

WHAT animals make sweet sounds and what animals make unpleasant sounds?

# Teacher Section

"Be not rash with thy mouth,
and let not thine heart
be hasty to utter
any thing before God."
Ecclesiastes 5:2

# INSTRUCTIONS
## For the Teacher

## Step 1

Study the Bible Lesson and begin to memorize the Memory Verses. Familiarize Yourself With the Character Quality. The student can answer the Bible Review Questions. See page 6. Use the Steps in Bible Study.

## Bible Lesson

**"The Fullness of Time"** – Ecclesiastes 3:1-15; Luke 1:26-35; Galatians 4:4, 5

## Memory Verses

Galatians 4:4-5; *The Desire of Ages* 32; Acts 3:22; Isaiah 61:1-3; 60:1-3; Genesis 49:10;  John 3:16-17

## Character Quality

**Alertness** – quick to understand and watching very carefully: vigilance; watchfulness; moving with celerity briskness; nimbleness; sprightliness

Antonyms – carelessness; indifference; unawareness; levity

**Character Quality Verse**

Mark 14:38 – *"Watch ye and pray, lest ye enter into temptation. The spirit truly is ready, but the flesh is weak."*

## Step 2

**Understand How To/And**

A. Do the Spelling Cards so the student can begin to build his own spiritual dictionary.

B. Mark the Bible.

C. Evaluate Your Student's Character in relation to the character quality of **alertness**.

D. Familiarize Yourself With the Voice Culture. Notice the Projects.

E. Review the Scripture References from the Student Section.

F. Notice the Answer Key.

# A. Spelling Cards

## Spelling Lists

**Voice Words**
**Place II - III**
animal
breath
breathing
deep
degree
emotions
mind
sound
spoken
sung
visible
invisible

**Place II - III**
character
communicated
consecrate
disposition
glorifying
influence
intelligence
pleasing
privileges
technique
unique

**Bible Words**
adoption
**alert**
**alertness**
blessed

**Bible Words**
**continued**
conceive
David
end
espoused
faileth
favour (favor)
favoured
forever
fullness
Galilee
Israel
Jesus
Joseph
kingdom
law
made
Mary
Nazareth
prolonged
proverb
redeem
reign
sent
sons (Son)
stand
throne
time
troubled
under
virgin
vision

# B. How to Mark the Bible

1. Copy the list of Bible texts in the back of the Bible on an empty page as a guide.

2. Go to the first text in the Bible and copy the next text beside it. Go to the next one and repeat the process until they are all chain referenced.

3. Have the student present the study to family and/or friends.

4. In this student lesson collect the Bible verses. And make your own Bible study. Mark your Bible.

# C. Evaluate Your Student's Character

This section is for the purpose of helping the teacher know how to encourage the students in becoming more **alert**.

See page 7.

> **See *Spelling From the Scriptures* for instructions about the Spelling Cards.**

# D. Familiarize Yourself With Voice Culture
## Notice the Projects

# Projects

1. Practice the principles learned in this lesson when talking. Be **alert**!

2. Take a walk as a family and find something in nature that is **alert** to God's plan for it. Discuss as a family what you found, and also what might happen if it was not **alert** to God's plan.

3. Have the student read the last paragraph of *The Desire of Ages* on page 297. Have him explain to the rest of the family what this paragraph is saying. Remind him to be **alert** and to think it out.

4. Have the student explain what discipline has to do with the talent of voice. Remind him to be **alert** and explain all he can.

5. Have the student make a poster listing the following five words: devotion, direction, discipline,

diligence, and discerning (**alertness**). Have him define each word and display it where he can see it every day until Lesson 3 is completed in all subjects.

### Was Israel **alert** to God's Instructions?

Place I = Grades 2-3-4
Place II = Grades 4-5-6
Place III = Grades 6-7-8

# E. Review the Scripture References from the Student Section

See the Student Section, and check all the Bible verses listed there.

# F. Notice the Answer Key

The Answer Key for the student book is found on page 9.

## Step 3

**Read the Lesson Aim.**

# Lesson Aim

The purpose of this lesson is to gain an understanding that God has given us an instrument that we must learn to use correctly in order to speak and sing in harmony with heaven.

This lesson will encourage correct speaking and singing. The student will need to be **alert** when practicing so that they will always use a correct technique, or damage can result to the vocal cords.

*"Be sober, be vigilant [alert]; because your adversary the devil, as a roaring lion, walketh about, seeking whom he may devour"* (I Peter 5:8).

God gave men His word to guide them. He laid out the foundation of His law that they could live in harmony with Him. He gave them the prophets to foretell the future that they could discern the times.

God's people, even though they had all of these instructions, were not **alert** to them. They did not correctly discern His words. "As the Jews had departed from God, faith had grown dim, and hope had well-nigh ceased to illuminate the future. The words of the prophets were uncomprehended."*

When no more could be done in that current situation, God sent His Son to the human family when the fullness of the time came. "...Christ must come to utter words which should be clearly and definitely understood."**

> "The words of the prophets were uncomprehended."

*The Desire of Ages 32  **The Desire of Ages 34*

Christ was the perfect example lived out in humanity. He used His voice correctly in speech and song. We must be **alert** to the instructions laid out for us in God's word for our voices so that we do not damage them. Whenever we damage a part of our bodies, we lessen our ability to serve God.

The voice is a part of the image of God in humanity. During the time of our Bible lesson, "Satan was exulting that he had succeeded in debasing the image of God in humanity."* As we learn to speak correctly and seek God's Spirit, our words will be used by God to give a message that will prepare souls for Christ's second coming. Are we **alert** to our responsibility to be a mouthpiece for God?

## Notes

*The Desire of Ages 37*

# Step 4

**Prepare to begin the Voice Culture Lesson.**

## To Begin the Voice Lesson

Interview someone who has a very pleasing speaking voice. Find out if he had any special training. If so, what was it? or Read the story, "What a Little Girl Said to a King."

# Step 5

**Begin the Voice Culture lesson. Cover only what can be understood by your student. Make the lesson a family project by all being involved in part or all of the lesson. These lessons are designed for the whole family.**

# Steps in Bible Study

1. Prayer

2. Read the verses/meditate/memorize.

3. Look up key words in *Strong's Concordance* and find their meaning in the Hebrew or Greek dictionary in the back of that book.

4. Cross reference (marginal reference) with other Bible texts. An excellent study tool is *The Treasury of Scripture Knowledge.*

5. Use Bible custom books for more information on the times.

6. Write a summary of what you have learned from those verses.

7. Mark key thoughts in the margin of your Bible.

8. Share your study with others to reinforce the lessons you have learned.

# Review Questions

1. Does God have a time table? (Ecclesiastes 3:1-15)

2. To whom was the angel Gabriel sent? (Luke 1:26-27)

3. In what town did Mary live? (Luke 1:26)

4. Who was to be Mary's husband? (Luke 1:27)

5. How did the angel greet Mary? (Luke 1:28)

6. What did the angel say to remove her fear? (Luke 1:29-30)

7. Who did the angel say should be born to her? (Luke 1:31-33)

8. What does "Jesus" mean? (See a concordance.)

9. What did the angel say of Jesus' throne and kingdom? (Luke 1:32-33)

10. What would He be called? (Luke 1:31)

11. When did God send His Son to this earth? (Galatians 4:4)

12. What does it mean *"the fullness of time had come?"* In God's reckoning or man's?

**Thought Question:** Why was it necessary for Christ to come to earth as a man to save man? (He came to fulfil what Adam failed to do in the flesh, and He lived a perfect example of righteousness.)

# Evaluating Your Child's Character

Check the appropriate box for your student's level of development,
or your own, as the case may be.

Maturing Nicely (MN), Needs Improvement (NI), Poorly Developed (PD), Absent (A)

## Alertness

1. Does the child show **alertness** and recognize opportunities and dangers on his own?

MN  NI  PD  A
☐   ☐   ☐   ☐

2. Is the child able to visualize the consequences of subtle dangers and act according to the wisdom of Scripture? *"A prudent man forseeth the evil, and hideth himself"* (Proverbs 22:3).

MN  NI  PD  A
☐   ☐   ☐   ☐

3. Does the child act quickly upon command?

MN  NI  PD  A
☐   ☐   ☐   ☐

4. Is the child sluggish in the morning?

Yes      No
☐        ☐

5. Is the child **alert** to the special needs of others about him?

MN  NI  PD  A
☐   ☐   ☐   ☐

## Notes

# WHat A Little Girl Said to A King

The King of Prussia, while visiting a village in his dominions, was welcomed by the school children of the palace. After their speaker had made a speech for them, he thanked them. Then, taking an orange from a plate, he asked:

"To what kingdom does this belong?"

"The vegetable kingdom sir," replied a little girl.

The king took a coin from his pocket and, holding it up, asked "And to what kingdom does this belong?"

"To the mineral kingdom," said the girl.

"And to what kingdom do I belong, then?" queried the king.

The little girl blushed deeply, for she did not want to say "the animal kingdom," as he expected she would, lest his majesty should be offended. Just then it flashed into her mind that *"God made man in his own image,"* and looking up with a brightening eye, she said:

"To God's kingdom, sir."

The king was deeply moved. A tear stood in his eye. He placed his hand upon the child's head, and said, most devoutly:

"God grant that I may be accounted worthy of that kingdom!"

Thus did the words of a child move the heart of a king. Let children learn from this that even their words may do either good or harm. A cross word from a child may wound the heart of a mother, a loving one, may make it glad. Children, let your words be kind, true, and right. Always be **alert** to the possibility of being the mouthpiece of God's Spirit.

> "God grant that I may be accounted worthy of that kingdom!"

# Answer Key

## Page 3

1. Mind

2. Spirit

3. Thoughts

4. Shallow thinking, shallow breathing

5. Mind

6. Joyful thoughts

7. Anger

8. Sympathy and tenderness

9. The person rushes through the act of expressing his ideas. They do not breath often enough.

## Page 7

1. A turtle dove has a sweet song and a sweet disposition or a crow has a discordant voice and an aggressive disposition.

2. Tone

3. Truth

4. Character

# Alertness Quotes

Choose several quotes and make posters
to hang in appropriate places in your home.
What do each of these quotes teach about <u>alertness</u>?

"Be always vigilant;
there are many snares
for the good."
—Accius 100 B.C.

"Warned of my foe,
I shun my foe."
—Timothy Kendall 1577

"The garrison is stronger
when it is long-time
advised."
—Chaucer 1387

"Good watch prevents
misfortune."
—English Proverb

"Observation, not old age,
brings wisdom."
—Publilius Syrus 43 B.C.

"The wise man
does at once
what the fool does finally."
—Baltasar Gracian

"Seeing many things,
but thou observest not;
opening the ears,
but he heareth not."
Isaiah 42:20

"The ox knoweth
his owner,
and the ass
his master's crib:
but Israel doth not know,
my people doth not
consider."
Isaiah 1:3

"Whoso is wise,
and will observe
these things,
even they
shall understand
the lovingkindness
of the Lord."
Psalm 107:43

# Gardening Sheet

Lesson  Three          Subject  Voice
Title  "Voice Culture"

| In Season | Out of Season |
|---|---|

**(This can be for both
In Season and Out of Season.)**

Explain to the family (or
friends) the importance of analyzing
the soil and how it can be done.

Use your voice correctly when
speaking. Be **alert** to answer any
questions. If you cannot answer
them, find out the answers and then
return to them with the information.

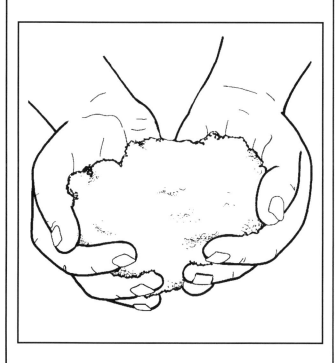

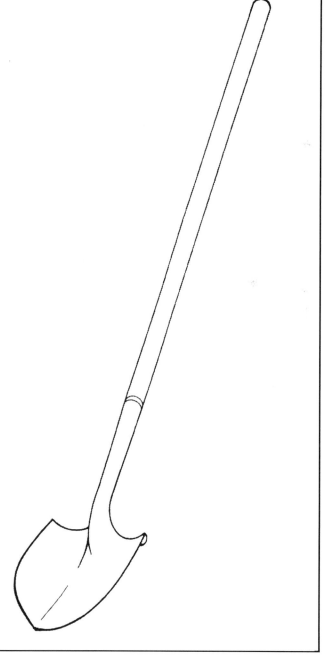

# Student
# Section

# "A soft answer turneth away wrath: but grievous words stir up anger."
## Proverbs 15:1

# Voice Culture

 ## Research
### Influence

"I will sing of the mercies of the Lord for ever: with my mouth will I make known they faithfulness to all generations."
Psalm 89:1

In our study of the different things that are involved in producing a pleasing voice, we will be looking at the correct way of using the different body parts that are involved. But, before we go into these details of technique, it is important for us to consider the influence of the mind and heart on what is spoken or sung.

Our voice is to be used in glorifying God. *"I will sing of the mercies of the Lord for ever: with my mouth will I make known they faithfulness to all generations"* (Psalm 89:1). "The messenger of the covenant" desires to speak through us in these last days. "The message of salvation is communicated to men through human agencies."* Are we **alert** to our responsibilities and privileges? Will we succeed where the Jews failed in being God's voice in the world?

*The Desire of Ages 36

The human voice is one of the special ways we have been given to "advertise" God's character. And to the degree that we know Him and partake of His Spirit, to that degree we can make Him known through our voices.

Our voice is to be used in glorifying God.

## The Voice and the Mind

In our previous lessons, we saw how the unique sound of each person's voice is related to the size and shape of the different body parts involved in the production of sound. And, while the voice bears a direct and important relation to the body, it also bears an indirect, but important, relation to the mind. The body is visible while the mind is invisible; but, without the mind, a person's voice would lack expression. A person's intelligence is expressed by their voice. Deep breathing and deep thoughts go together in producing deep, musical voices, both in speaking and singing. On the other hand, shallow thinking and shallow breathing combine in producing a shallow, empty, disagreeable, monotonous voice. This is the kind of voice that many of the rabbis had in Christ's day. Their lack of spirituality affected their voice quality.

A healthy mind is just as important in producing a nice voice as is a healthy body. An **alert** mind thinks clearly, feels deeply, and wills decidedly. Unclear thinking, empty feeling, and hesitation in making decisions go along with voice disability.

## Character

The mind, and the emotions it produces, give character to the voice. For example, anger tends to constrict the voice, making it sound throaty and disagreeable, while sympathy and tenderness make the voice softer, richer, and more pleasant to the ear. Joyful thoughts make the voice purer and cause an expansion of the body. This produces a corresponding openness of the throat and freedom of tone.

The **alert** observer can often tell a person's profession simply by the tones of the voice. For instance, public speakers sometimes develop a habit of speaking forced and loud tones because they think the effort is necessary to be heard. As a general rule, the voice of a person show their habits, trends of mind, convictions, and emotions.

A Healthy mind is just as important in producing a nice voice as is a Healthy body.

Some of the worst voice defects are the result of mental and emotional actions. An example of a fault of this kind is when a person does not breath often enough when they are speaking. This happens when the speaker is mentally anxious to rush through the act of expressing his ideas. He may be thinking the complete thought he is about to utter, or he may be thinking way ahead of the phrase he is speaking. Whatever is motivating him to speak hurriedly, if he slows his mind down so that he is thinking only one thing at a time, and concentrates on realizing each impression, then his breathing will become easy, natural and more frequent. His voice will also become much more expressive. *"Be not rash with thy mouth, and let not thine heart be hasty to utter any thing before God"* (Ecclesiastes 5:2). Remember, when you are tempted to interrupt others or to used hurried speech that "God's purposes know no haste..."*

> "Be not rash
> with thy mouth,
> and let not thine heart
> be hasty to utter
> any thing before God."
> Ecclesiastes 5:2

*The Desire of Ages 32*

# Review

1. Besides the vocal organs themselves, what influences the voice?

2. To the degree that we partake of God's _ _ _ _ _ _ , to that degree we can make Him known through our voices.

3. Deep _ _ _ _ _ _ _ _ and deep breathing go together in producing deep, musical voices.

4. What is one cause of a monotonous voice?

5. The _ _ _ _ gives character to the voice.

6. What emotion produces openness of the throat and freedom of tone?

7. What emotion constricts the voice?

8. What emotions make the voice soft and rich?

9. If a person is in a hurried state of mind how does it affect his manner of talking?

# Reinforce

1. Notice peoples' voices. Does the sound of their voice ever give you a clue as to what kind of a job they have?

2. Practice taking deep breaths before speaking when you are feeling anxious.

## The Sound Birds Make Tell About Their Character

Dove

Blue Jay

# Research

## Animal Voices
"...Let me hear thy voice; for sweet is thy voice...."
Song of Solomon 2:14

The relationship between character and voice can also be seen in the animal kingdom. Animals with voices are usually of a higher order and have more refined feelings than those without voices. The character of the animal being revealed by the voice can be proven by the fact that the birds having the gentlest dispositions, such as the turtle dove, have the sweetest songs. Blue jays, English sparrows, crows, hawks and other "robbers" make unpleasant, discordant sounds.

Is your voice sweet or discordant?

# Emotions

## "To this end was I born,
## and for this cause came I into the world,
## that I should bear witness unto the truth.
## Every one that is of the truth heareth my voice."
### John 18:37

Any negative emotion affects the quality of tone in a person's voice. You can notice this as you listen to people talk when they are in pain, or afraid. Positive emotions naturally improve the quality of the tones.

As God's people are called to be mouth pieces for Him, you can see how they must have the proper emotions and thoughts to back up the words they speak. Their voices will have more power for good in the world as mind, words, and tones unite in true harmony.

Let us dedicate our voices for the purpose of expressing truth and righteousness. In order to carry this desire out, the mind must be fortified against the evil, the ugly, and the false.

*"Whatsoever things are true, whatsoever things are honest, whatsoever things are just, whatsoever things are pure, whatsoever things are lovely, whatsoever things are of good report; if there be any virtue, and if there be any praise, think on these things"* (Philippians 4:8).

# More Power

God's peoples' voices will have more power for good in the world as mind, words, and tones unite in true harmony.

As we consecrate our voices to God we may humbly say with Jesus, *"To this end was I born, and for this cause came I into the world, that I should bear witness unto the truth. Every one that is of the truth heareth my voice"* (John 18:37).

Our goal concerning our voice is to be like Christ, our great Example. His mind, His actions, and His words all harmonized. "What He taught, He lived....thus in His life, Christ's words had perfect illustration and support. And more than this; what He taught, He was. His words were the expression not only of His own experience, but of His own character. Not only did He teach the truth, but He was the truth. It was this that gave His teaching power."*

*"And it came to pass when Jesus had ended these sayings, the people were astonished at his doctrine, for he taught them as one having authority, and not as the scribes"* (Matthew 7:28-29).

# Christ's mind, actions, and words Harmonized.

"What He taught, He lived....thus in His life, Christ's words had perfect illustration and support. And more than this; what He taught, He was."

*Education 78-79

And so, the first steps to be taken in voice culture are with the heart and soul. And, once this is begun, there is good hope of progress along the lines of the physical development of the vocal organs. We will be learning in the following lessons how to exercise the bodily organs in such a way as to produce the most melodious voice possible. In the meantime, remember the exercise recommended by the apostle Paul, *"Exercise thyself rather unto godliness. For bodily exercise profiteth little; but godliness is profitable unto all things"* (I Timothy 4:7-8).

Remember,
the first steps
to be taken
in voice culture
are with
the heart and soul.

"And it came to pass when Jesus had ended these sayings, the people were astonished at His doctrine,

"For He taught them as one having authority, and not as the scribes." Matthew 7:28-29

## Review

1. Give an example of how an animal's character is expressed by the type of voice it has.



2. Emotions affect the __ __ __ __ of a person's voice.



3. Our voices are for bearing *"witness unto the* __ __ __ __ __ *."*



4. Words have power only as they are the expression of a person's true

__ __ __ __ __ __ __ __ __ __ .

# Reinforce

1. Go for a nature walk and be **alert** especially to animals' voices. Did you hear any of the birds' voices mentioned in this lesson?

**Flicker**

**Kingbird**

2. Be **alert** to the sound of peoples' voices. Can you tell what emotion they are feeling when they talk? Can you think of a Bible text that tells you how to talk to a person who is angry? (See Proverbs 15:1.)

3. When it is your turn to read a Scripture in family worship, try to make your tone of voice express the thoughts of the text instead of reading monotonously.

"A soft answer turneth away wrath: but grievous words stir up anger."
Proverbs 15:1

"By long forbearing is a prince persuaded, and a soft tongue breaketh the bone."
Proverbs 25:15

# Outline of School Program

| Age | Grade | Program |
|---|---|---|
| Birth through Age 7 | Babies Kindergarten and Pre-school | *Family Bible Lessons* (This includes: Bible, Science–Nature, and Character) |
| Age 8 | First Grade | *Family Bible Lessons* (This includes: Bible, Science–Nature, and Character) + Language Program (*Writing and Spelling Road to Reading and Thinking* [WSRRT]) |
| Age 9-14 or 15 | Second through Eighth Grade | *The Desire of all Nations* (This includes: Health, Mathematics, Music, Science–Nature, History/Geography/Prophecy, Language, and Voice–Speech) + Continue using WSRRT |
| Ages 15 or 16-19 | Ninth through Twelfth Grade | 9 – *Cross and Its Shadow I** + Appropriate Academic Books<br><br>10 – *Cross and Its Shadow II** + Appropriate Academic Books<br><br>11 – *Daniel the Prophet** + Appropriate Academic Books<br><br>12 – *The Seer of Patmos** (Revelation) + Appropriate Academic Books<br><br>*or you could continue using *The Desire of Ages* |
| Ages 20-25 | College | Apprenticeship |

Made in the USA
Monee, IL
21 August 2022